THE FAMILY PROCLAMATION

...AND YOU

Written and
Illustrated by
David Bowman

"True doctrine, understood, changes attitudes and behavior"
- Elder Boyd K. Packer

Why **The Firmly Founded Series**?

Today's LDS children are amazing! Have you noticed? ☺
They come to earth with a pre-mortal fire of faith just waiting to be stoked. I believe they are ready to be taught the pure, core doctrines of our church… but still in the fun, visually-engaging language of children.
I have focused an entire book on the Family Proclamation because it is such a core doctrine
and so needed today!

I hope these books can be an effective tool in helping you teach these young, valiant souls…
or for anyone who still likes to learn with pictures ☺

God Bless,

David Bowman

ISBN: 978-1-62972-371-6
SKU: 5182490

Printed in China
R. R. Donnelley & Sons, Shenzhen, China
10 9 8 7 6 5 4 3 2 1

Author's Note

This book is a *companion* (not a replacement) to your family's study of "The Family: A Proclamation to the World," to help your kids further understand, appreciate, and internalize its concepts.

Fun rhyming phrases (based on the acronym **I AM FAMILY PROC**) help summarize the order and content of each paragraph of The Family Proclamation.

As in all my books, application is the focus! In this book, the colored pages show ways your kids can follow the nine principles of successful families found in The Family Proclamation.

FHE lesson helps in the back include teaching ideas, links to great lds.org resources, and a summary of the **I AM FAMILY PROC** rhymes to put on your fridge.

Happy learning! ☺

David Bowman

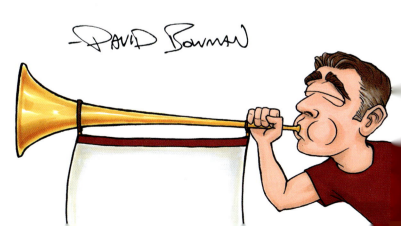

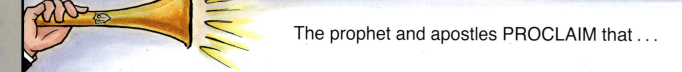

The prophet and apostles PROCLAIM that . . .

MARRIAGE & FAMILY

are

CENTRAL

to Heavenly Father's Great Plan of Happiness!

IN GOD'S PLAN, IT'S ALL ABOUT FAM

Paragraph 1
"WE THE FIRST PRESIDENCY . . ."

Everyone is a
**spirit son or daughter
of heavenly parents.**
That makes us all one big family, created
in the image of God! Boys have always been
boys and girls have always been girls.

Your gender is part of who you are.

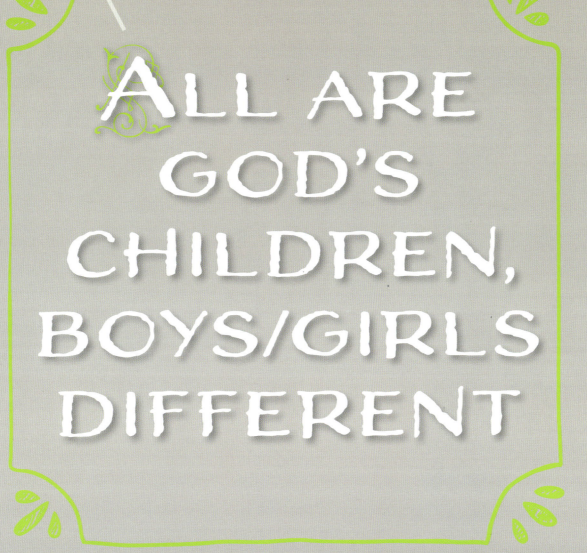

ALL ARE GOD'S CHILDREN, BOYS/GIRLS DIFFERENT

Paragraph 2
"ALL HUMAN BEINGS. . ."

Before we were born, we knew and loved our Heavenly Father. He presented a plan that would help us to become as He is. It is called the Plan of Salvation or the **Great Plan of Happiness.**

In Heavenly Father's plan, each of us would go to earth and receive a physical body. Hooray!

While we are here on earth (and always), our greatest joys come from being part of a family.
So, we are born into families,
we are raised in families,

and then we start families of our own.

That's what life is all about . . . Families! ☺

I AM FAMILY PROC

MORTAL BIRTH, START PROGRESS ON EARTH

Paragraph 3 (1st half)
"IN THE PREMORTAL REALM. . ."

FOREVER THOSE FEELINGS, WITH TEMPLE SEALINGS

Paragraph 3 (2nd half)
"The divine plan. . ."

Adam and Eve were the first man and woman on earth.

In the Garden of Eden, Heavenly Father gave them a very, VERY, <u>VERY</u> important commandment:

"Multiply and replenish the earth."

In other words:
Have babies and start a family!

Because Adam and Eve were married, they had God's permission to become parents.

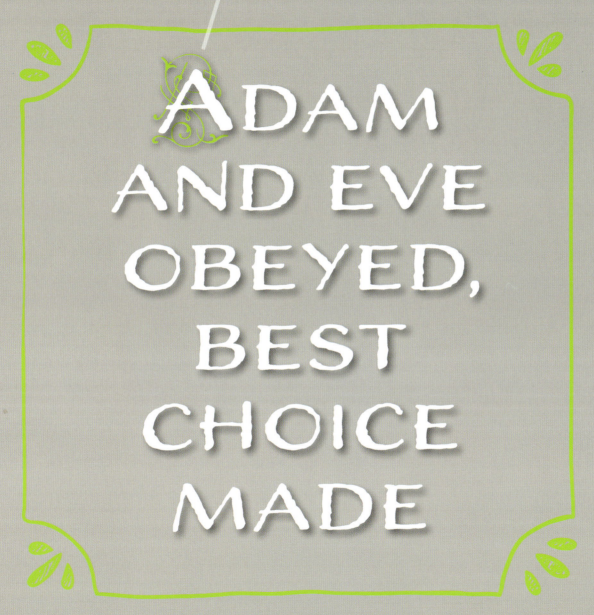

ADAM AND EVE OBEYED, BEST CHOICE MADE

Paragraph 4
"THE FIRST COMMANDMENT. . ."

From Adam and Eve until today, each time a baby is born, it allows one of Heavenly Father's spirit children to come to earth and get a body.

It's how YOU came to earth and got YOUR body! ☺ Triple Hooray!

This power to create a baby is very sacred.
God commands that **only married husbands and wives use this power**. Why??

Married man and wife, together make life

Paragraph 5
"WE DECLARE. . ."

. . .And what a big job too!

Parents teach their children to obey God's commandments.

They show them how to love and serve others.

They take care of their needs and prepare them to be responsible, grown-ups someday.

I AM FAMILY PROC

It's not easy. Mom and Dad need your help!

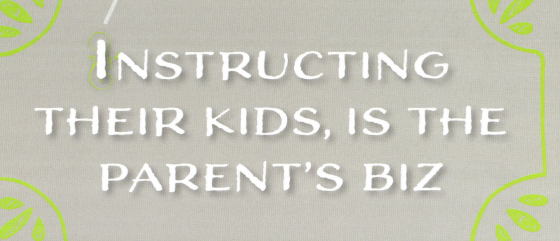

INSTRUCTING THEIR KIDS, IS THE PARENT'S BIZ

Paragraph 6
"HUSBAND AND WIFE. . ."

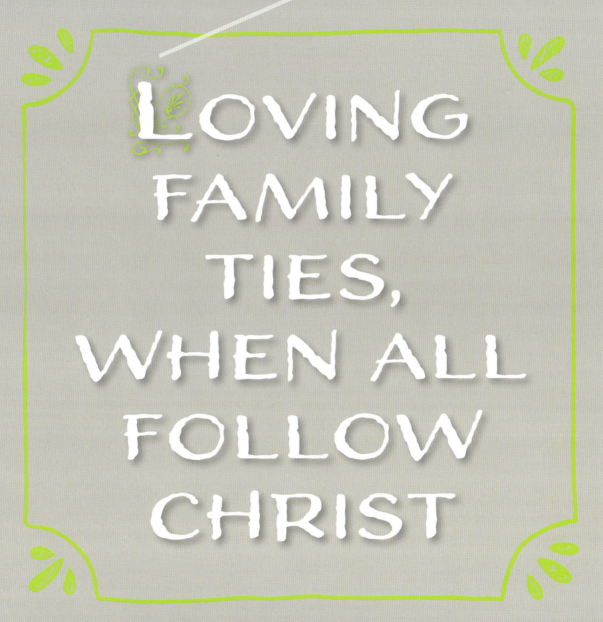

LOVING FAMILY TIES, WHEN ALL FOLLOW CHRIST

Paragraph 7 (part 1)
"THE FAMILY IS. . ."

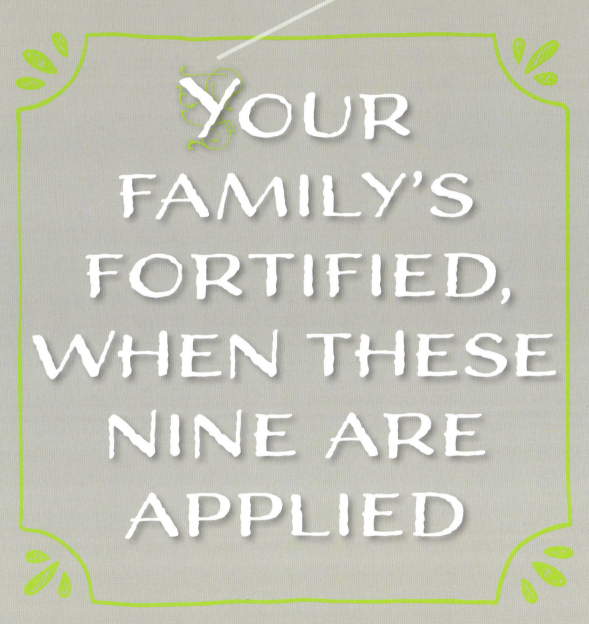

YOUR FAMILY'S FORTIFIED, WHEN THESE NINE ARE APPLIED

Paragraph 7 (part 2)
"Successful marriages and families are established and maintained on principles of..."

1

FORTIFY YOUR family through . . .
FAITH

Put God first in your family! That means read the scriptures together (even if they're hard to understand sometimes), have family home evenings, go to church, and pray together. Keep things out of your home that don't bring the spirit . . . like certain movies, TV shows, video games, and websites. I know it can be hard sometimes to do all these things cheerfully, **but you can do hard things!** ☺

2

FORTIFY YOUR family through . . .
PRAYER

Pray together as a family often. Kneel down, fold your arms, close your eyes, and bow your head. When it's YOUR turn to pray, how great is that! Enjoy talking with Heavenly Father! When it's not your turn, listen carefully to whoever is praying. Try to feel that calm feeling of the Holy Ghost whenever your family prays together. I know it's hard sometimes to stay reverent for an ENTIRE prayer, **but you can do hard things!** ☺

3

FORTIFY YOUR family through . . .
REPENTANCE

In families, everyone is going to make mistakes (even moms and dads). Teasing your sister, getting angry and yelling at your brother, talking back to mom and dad . . . Jesus did not teach these things. So, when you make a mistake, say you're sorry (and really mean it too). Try to make things better to those you hurt by showing extra love. I know it can be hard to get a soft heart when you're just soooo mad, **but you can do hard things!** ☺

4

FORTIFY YOUR family through . . .
FORGIVENESS

And if someone in your family does something mean or annoying or unfair to you . . . do you get angry back at them? No, siree! Jesus taught us to always treat others the way we want to be treated. That means we forgive them . . . even if they didn't say sorry. I know that can be hard to do sometimes, **but you can do hard things!** ☺

5

FORTIFY YOUR family through . . .
RESPECT

Each member of your family deserves respect. Treat them the same way you treat your best friends. Use kind voices with each other. Use good manners. Don't take other's things without asking. Follow the family rules. Do what your parents ask you to do the FIRST time without complaining. That shows your mom and dad respect. Are these things hard to do sometimes? Sure. **But, you can do hard things!** ☺

6

FORTIFY YOUR family through . . .
LOVE

Jesus taught us to "love one another" the same way He loves us. That is especially important at home. Do a kind service for your brother. Give your sister a big hug and tell her you love her. Help your mom without being asked. Give your dad a neck scratch (he loves that ☺). Each time you show love to each other, you will feel a warm fuzzy inside. I know showing love can be hard to remember sometimes, **but you can do hard things!** ☺

7

FORTIFY YOUR family through . . .
COMPASSION

Compassion is that feeling you get when you care more about someone else than yourself. Notice when a family member is sad and then cheer them up. Notice your baby brother or sister and play with them. Think of others by letting them have the first turn. Remember that caring about people (especially your family) is most important. When you remember Jesus' example, **I know you can do this hard thing!** ☺

FORTIFY YOUR family through . . .
WORK

Work is awesome! Do your chores happily. Do your morning and nighttime routines without being asked. Help Mom in the house. Help Dad in the yard. Do a good job and stick to the job until it's done. Don't be afraid to work! Don't whine. Don't be a Laman and Lemuel. Hard work feels good when you have the right attitude. I know this can be hard to remember, but . . . you guessed it! **You can do hard work!** ☺

9

FORTIFY YOUR family through . . .
WHOLESOME RECREATIONAL ACTIVITIES

And always remember . . . Families are FUN! ☺☺☺
Have a good time together. Laugh a lot! Play games. It
doesn't matter who wins, just enjoy being together. Plan
fun family activities, like going to the park or camping.
I know having fun as a family can be really hard
sometimes, but . . . just kidding! **This one is easy!** ☺

Did you know that Heavenly Father designed dads and moms to have **different** roles in families?

DAD's job is to provide

for his family. That means he goes to work to earn $$$ so his family can have food, clothing, and a place to live. He protects his family. He presides and gives priesthood blessings.

MOM's job is to nurture

the children. That means she takes care of them and focuses on their needs first. Teaching her children is a mother's greatest work!

Dads and moms are *equal partners* in raising their families.
They work together as a team!

PARENTS ARE WHOLE, WHEN EACH DOES THEIR ROLE

Paragraph 7 (part 3)
"By divine design. . ."

However, not all homes have a mom *and* a dad. Sometimes sad things happen like death or divorce. Sometimes parents can't do their roles completely. Grandparents and others can be great helps. Remember . . . **Heavenly Father loves <u>all</u> families, even if things are hard.**

And, with God's help . . . we can all do hard things.

ROUGH TIMES? FEELING TRAPPED? FAMILIES CAN ADAPT

Paragraph 7 (part 4)
"Disability, death. . ."

OH, JUDGMENT'S ASSURED, IF THIS WARNING'S NOT HEARD

Paragraph 8
"WE WARN. . ."

CALL UPON ALL, TO HELP FAMILIES STAND TALL

Paragraph 9
"WE CALL UPON. . ."

I drew my family on the cover of this book ... now, its your turn to draw YOUR **FORCE FIELD**, **FORTIFIED** family below! (You can draw the whole family yourself OR each person in the family can draw themselves)

WHINE

ARGUIN

RESPECT

FORGIVENESS

REPENTANCE

PRAYER

FAITH

LOVE

COMPASSION

WORK

WRA

YOUR FAMILY'S FORTIFIED, WHEN THESE NINE ARE APPLIED

FORTIFIED

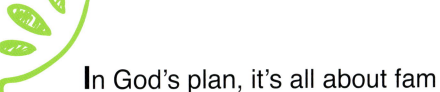

In God's plan, it's all about fam

All are God's children, boys/girls different
Mortal birth, start progress on earth

Forever those feelings, with temple sealings
Adam and Eve obeyed, best choice made
Married man and wife, together make life
Instructing their kids, is the parent's biz
Loving family ties, when all follow Christ
Your family's fortified, when these 9 are applied!

Parents are whole, when each does their role
Rough times? Feeling trapped? Families can adapt
Oh, judgment's assured, if this warning's not heard
Call upon all, to help families stand tall

Family Proclamation—FHE LESSON HELPS

There is a vast amount of resources available online for teaching the Family Proclamation and its doctrines to your family...

especially on www.lds.org:

• In 2017, each *Ensign* magazine has an idea for teaching The Family Proclamation. To find all of them, go to lds.org and search: **ProclamationKids**

• For more great helps, go to **lds.org/children/resources**.
   click—**Home and Family** (bottom left)
      click—The Family: A Proclamation to the World or Happiness in Family Life
   You can also click—**Lesson Helps for Teaching Children**, then
      click—Lesson Helps by Topic. You will find several topic that are found in the Proclamation, including most of the 9 Principles of Successful Families (the Force Fields).

And since these 9 principles really are the rubber-meets-the-road applications of this book, here are some more activity ideas I came up with/found for each of these 9:

FAITH—*IN THE WATER, BUT NOT OF THE WATER*

This is a great object lesson from the New Era, January 2017:
   https://www.lds.org/new-era/2017/01/what-are-you-doing-to-stay-dry?lang=eng

Basically, fill a large pitcher with water. The goal?—Submerge a paper towel without it getting wet. Tools?—a plastic cup and tape. How?—Fold up paper towel til its a small square shape, tape it to the inside/bottom of cup, turn cup upside down and completely submerge cup in water. Air pocket stays in cup, paper towel stays dry and kids are incredulous (mine sure were)! Then, help the kids explain how the water is the world, the paper towel is us, the cup is the faithful gospel things we do (you know... the list :), and the tape is our commitment to DOING those things. Remember: Let the kiddos make the analogy applications while you ask the right questions, don't just tell them everything.

PRAYER—*CHARGE IT!*

Show the kids your smart phone and some of the neat things it can do. Then, show them the plug-in charger and ask why this is so important. What happens if you don't charge it? How long will a charge last? Help them to explain how this phone charger is like prayer (Ex: We are the phone. Without continuous connections with God (the outlet) through prayer (the charger/chord), our power/abilities decline. We need regular recharges. And "going through the motions" of prayer without meaning it is like plugging our phones into the chord (prayer), but not plugging the chord into the outlet (God). Doesn't do much good.

To help kids have more MEANINGFUL prayers, try "BECAUSE PRAYERS" (See Who's Your Hero? Vol. 1 - Enos). Basically, whoever is praying says the word "because" at the end of each sentence of the prayer, and then he/she tells Heavenly Father the reason why he/she is thanking Him for that blessing or asking him for that request. Watch your kids start to really think about why they say the things they say while praying.

REPENTANCE—*HOW WE SAY SORRY*

Here's a great way to help your kids understand what apologizing REALLY is (not the meaningless "forced" apology we all love to force).

Make a sign titled: **HOW WE SAY SORRY**. Below, write these four steps. Discuss and role-play:

I'm sorry for... (Be specific, and recognize what you did that was wrong)
This was wrong because... (Show you understand how you hurt the other person)
In the future I will... (Find a positive statement ("I will"... not "I won't") for what you can do in the future)
Optional step: **How can I make it better?...** (Offender offers a way he/she can make amends)
Will you forgive me?... (Ask for the other persons forgiveness)
   (see http://www.techiechic.net/blog/saying-sorry-fhe/ for more info on this)

FORGIVENESS—*FORGIVEN AND FORGOTTEN*

I's amazing how much easier the forgiveness will happen, if family members follow the "REPENTANCE: How We Say Sorry" steps above. To practice this process of REPENTANCE and FORGIVENESS...

On small sheets of note paper, family members write down things that they sometimes do that makes others in the family unhappy or upset. Then, he/she gives that paper to the person they hurt. Family members takes turns reading each one. After each "offence" is read, the person who wrote it follows the HOW WE SAY SORRY steps to that person.

When he/she is finished, the person holding the paper then tears up the paper and says with a smile, "Yes, I can forgive you!" and gives the other person a big ol' hug! When finished, go outside and bury all the paper shreds (or burn them up). Forgiven and forgotten!

RESPECT—*FIND OUT WHAT IT MEANS TO ME?*

This is a hard concept for kids to understand, so defining "Respect" by simply giving concrete examples of *what it is* and *what it is not* probably works best. Synonyms: *"polite, reverent, courteous, good-manners."* Opposites: *"rude, selfish, loud, unkind."*

Write common situations on slips of paper and have kids draw each one out of a bowl. Then they explain what is respectful and disrespectful in these situations. Some situations might be:

HOME: mealtime, FHE and family prayer and family scripture time, bedtime—
  (interactions with parents, siblings)
SCHOOL: in classroom, on the playground, on the bus—
  (interactions with teachers, other adults, peers)
CHURCH: in the church building, sacrament meeting, primary—
  (interactions with family, leaders, teachers)

LOVE—*HOW DO I LOVE THEE? LET ME WRITE THE WAYS*

Each family member cuts out a large heart from a sheet of paper and writes his/her name on the top. Then, everyone sits in a circle and passes their heart one person to the right. Each person writes something he/she loves about the person who's name is on the top (older siblings/parents can help younger kids who can't write yet). After certain amount of time, everyone passes the heart again and it continues until you get your own heart back. Read and share what everyone wrote. Give each other hugs!

Variation on this: THE LOVE SEAT (See WYH 1—Ammon, or WYH 2—Jesus Christ) Basically, each person gets a turn sitting in a comfy chair while each family member says one thing he/she loves about him/her.

COMPASSION—*FILLED WITH IT!*

3 Nephi 17 is a perfect example of Christ showing compassion! Read and discuss it together as a family, especially vs. 5-10, where Jesus heals them because His "bowels are filled with compassion." There is a great 4 min. video that depicts this chapter as well—go to lds.org and search "My Joy is Full video"

WORK—*TIDY TIME!*

HURRY! Dad sets his stopwatch and the entire family rushes from room to room, cleaning/tidying that room as a group, until every room in the house is clean. I know, some boy's bedrooms may take until dawn, so modify it as needed. Make it fast and furious and fun! Play Lone Ranger music on your phone! Piggy back ride kids to each room! Whatever! If your family reaches the specified time goal, then you all get the FHE treat.

WHOLESOME RECREATIONAL ACTIVITIES

Do something fun together! Need I say more? ☺

About the Author/Illustrator

David Bowman loves his wife and five kids! For fun, the Bowman family loves camping together, hiking together, skiing together, playing games together, and going to the beach (although it's quite a drive because they live in Arizona). They also love Family Home Evenings, morning scripture study, and family prayer (especially when the youngest, Colton, prays about the most random things).

You can check out all of Dave's books at **www.whosyourhero.com**
and all of his Christ-centered fine art at **www.davidbowmanart.com**